RAMBLING THOUGHTS OF A TRAVELING TIKI MAN

By

DANNY LYNN

"THE TIKI MAN"

Dedication

This book is dedicated to my Dad,

Ernest C Lynn 1926-2012

Without his love and guidance carefully molding me into the man I
am none of this would be possible.

Acknowledgements

I would like thank all of the people in my life who have encouraged me and supported my writings over the years and who have started their day with me on this journey of life, thank you all so very much.

To all my family that have always been there for me over the years and helped mold me in the man I am, far from perfect and made many mistakes along the way, thank you for always being there.

To My Parents Ernest and Tina- Thank you so very much for always being there and pushing me to always be the best. Thank you for sharing your traveling stories with me and helping me to be the man I am. Without your love and support over the years life would seem empty.

John Buskell – Thank you for your friendship and for all the talks we had. Without your help this would not be possible. Remember, *"You never know what the tide will bring in"*

Andy and Sam Goforth- Thank you for being the best brothers any one person could ask for , you've both always been my hero's.

My one and only sister Judy- Thank you for putting up with me over the years as I know I didn't always make it easy, I love you.

The Tiki Bar Board Members, Dan and Brenda (Mom), Mike and Julie, Marc and Donna- Thank you for always being in my circle of my closest friends and for all the good times we've shared.

My Children Julie, Randy, Jeffery, Brad and Justin- Being a Dad I never thought would be my biggest accomplishment in life. I know I was not always there, Lord knows I made mistakes as all parents do but my whole life has been for you and I love all of you dearly even though being a Dad sometimes seems like the bad guy.

RAMBLING

THOUGHTS OF A

TRAVELING TIKI MAN

By

DANNY LYNN

"THE TIKI MAN"

Good Morning.

Meanwhile, back on reflection Island in Pittong Beach 2013 was a great year and can honestly say I smiled and laughed more than I didn't, I met some new awesome people along the way even as they seem to be just passing through my life through the journey of that year, made a lot of new friends, spent a lot of time with an awesome family and had a lot of fun. Looking at 2014 and the promises it holds I'm always reminded of just how fast things can change, and when you're looking or faced with the changes sometime you just have to say "It's for the best" and move on because opportunity's window only stays open for so long. I guess true friendship is about the most you can offer someone, what they choose to do with it is their choice, we all have choices. Keep chasing those dreams in 2014, change is good that's why we have a reset button pushed on New Year's Eve

Have a great day and a super New Year; see you on the flip flop

Good Morning.

Meanwhile back in the Greek islands of Mykonos How does one stay happy every morning?

This may not be the simplest of things because the fight is not out of us but within us. We need to play this with our minds and ensure that we get this right each and every day. It may seem easy but it's not, especially if you are going through a traumatic experience.

But otherwise, it is easier. You just need to refocus from the bad to the good. A happy life is a well spent life and you must try it not only for yourself but for others too. Because when you are happy, you have a better chance of making someone else happy.

Wish you a happy morning!

Have a great day

Good Morning

Meanwhile outside The Chocolate Bar, this is the time of the year where those New Year's resolutions and goals start becoming difficult why? Well people are afraid of change but never be afraid to change your vision, set new goals, and challenge yourself. Life is best experienced without boundaries; so live each day ceremoniously and when in doubt, order the pie and If you're still looking for that one person who can change your life, baby take a look in the mirror Have a great day.

Good Morning

Meanwhile, on the other side of the island in a corner café the subject of listening came up, you ever worked for someone or been in a relationship with someone who does all the talking thinking they know what you're thinking without ever asking you? Hmmm listening is a skill for you to learn, you have to listen; and for you to listen, you have to be silent.

Did you know that listen and silent are words formed from the same letters? Try not doing all the talking and you just might find the source of the problem.

 Have a great day warm weather is on the way.

Good Morning.

Meanwhile, at the surfside coffee shop over in the corner where the morning sun shines through the blinds throwing bars on the table the discussion of misery loves company came up, basically how people who aren't happy surly can't be happy when you are. Don't let anyone steal your joy.

You might not always be able to control a situation, but you can control how you react to it.

Don't give your power away to anyone. When you allow your happiness to depend on what someone else does or says, then you are giving your power away. You need to decide to stay positive and not let someone decide your happiness for you.
Have a great day.

The way to happiness depends on you.

Good Morning

Meanwhile, Monday down towards the end of the boardwalk next to the funny mirror that makes you look different sizes and shapes, there is a bench where the seagulls gather mainly waiting on food from the two ladies who sit there each morning to watch the sunrise on the beach.

The subject came up about why things happen to you, does everything happen for a reason as we often discard as an excuse because we know we really let it happen most of the time.

Life is like a puzzle. Everything that happens to us is just a piece of it. We may not seem to understand where to put it, but one thing is sure, it will make us whole, make us who we're supposed to be.

Have a great day.

You're the piece of the puzzle.

Good Morning!

Meanwhile, looking out on the water in the distance you can see how the choppy waters naturally push the sail boat along its way in silent motion of wood, sail and water. Inside the sail boat looking back at the distant shore at the man at the Tiki Bar by the beach, the two lovers laying back and a little tired from the sunshine of the day the subject of "If" came up, what if this happens? Or what if tomorrow you feel different? Or the popular "Will it always be this way?" as if to say the weekend and day in the sun unplanned was now somehow not as important.

We often spend so much time coping with problems along our path that we only have a dim or even inaccurate view of what's really important to us.

Hope sees the invisible, feels the intangible, and achieves the impossible. The sense of wonder that is our sixth sense I believe, can and often make you scared of what seems to be perfect, it comes with wisdom and quite honestly the idiots that have danced across your threshold. Nothing wrong with thinking it out BUT as the wise Tiki Man once said "control the fear never let the fear control you" take a leap of faith never back jump and live in the now not the land of "IF" Have a great day.

Good Morning.

Meanwhile in Myrtle Beach down close to the 2nd street pier south side there is a bar famously name "McAdoos's Beach Bar" where you can walk right in from the beach and sit down.

Along the right side of the bar as you walk in, a window looks straight out to the beach, when open the breeze of the ocean brings in the smell of coconut lotion, the sounds of the beach and the sound of an airplane flying over pulling a sign.

There to the left Captain John talks to his girl about how things use to be in the fishing business, to the right Maria who migrated from Boston sips on her glass of wine and thinks about what could've been if she had stayed and the boy she left there, In the middle of the bar sits the Tiki Man who is only smiling drinking his land shark ice cold beer looking out of the window to the ocean only thinking of the future.

Here is the problem with living in the past, you ever looked back and thought what an idiot I was? And one can never venture off into "what could've been land" and get lost there.

Never let your past experiences harm your future, your past can't be altered and your future doesn't deserve the punishment.

Have a great day.

Good Morning from Beautiful Chattanooga.

Meanwhile, back at the Backend café around the corner at
Rembrandts sipping on coffee the subject of doing things for others
and if they really appreciate it or not came up.

Remember that the greatest reward you get for your efforts is not
what you get for them, but what you become by them. Never
underestimate the power of a kind word, an unexpected act of
generosity, a courageous deed and always remind yourself on the
path of life, few signs are big or clear.

Just don't get fooled by the ones that say, "You can't get there from
here" Have a great day and go out be somebody today

Good Morning.

Meanwhile down in Mobile at The Pelican Reef early in the morning watching the sunrise over Mobile Bay, there the subject of confidence and building bridges came up and how important it is in everything you do.

The only thing that lies between you and your dreams is your belief and self-confidence. Don't ever allow other people to choose your dreams or make you work for theirs.

 Live life today as if it were your last, live life only on your terms, always remember confidence is not when you know all the answers, confidence is when you are ready for all the questions the best bridge between failure and success is a bridge called determination. Have a great day.

Good Morning.

Meanwhile, down in Spanish Fort watching the sun rise the topic of emotionally draining people came up, those from your past who pop up from time to time and try to steal your positive thoughts away. You know who they are and you know when it happens.

If you are consumed with someone that has a pity party for themselves or constantly playing the victim card, you need to run fast!!! If not, this will consume all your positive energy and you will lose focus on the good things life has to offer you.

Don't rob your life of your own happiness, never give anyone else the power over you, stay strong to your path and your future.

Have a great day.

Good Morning.

Meanwhile, down in St. Lawrence in what the locals call "the Gap" in beautiful Barbados' there is a place called Sugars Lounge, where if you take the path from the back door that leads to the beach you can watch the pink flamingos waking to the sunrise that makes them appear more orange then pink, there the subject came up about destiny.

Remember, it's the road you take that decides your destiny and not your destiny that decides the road you take, choose wisely.

Losers live in the past. Winners learn from the past and move in the right direction, always moving forward.

Have a great day.

Good Morning.

Meanwhile, back on the island at the little coffee shop in the morning, he walked to Blok Bar, a cafe-bar a block from Maricela, on a quiet corner shaded by birch trees. Without asking, the waitress brings out a long espresso, which he drank slowly under white umbrellas on a wooden deck. There the subject of staying true to YOUR dreams came up with the lady in the red hat.

We create mountains out stones because our minds have the power to create. Fortunately or unfortunately, it creates what we constantly feed it with. Impossibility builds impossibility and possibility builds positivity. When you are faced with a seemingly "impossible" situation, don't worry; just find an eraser and erase the 'I and M and you will see Possible.

Have a great day.

Good Morning.

Meanwhile, at Lillie's Coffee Bar located between lemon and orange streets just off the coast in beautiful Neptune Florida, there in the back is a court yard where bright blue and yellow umbrellas cover old tables. You can sit and watch the sea planes land on the water bringing in the ice packed catch of the day from Boston and surrounding areas of Florida.

Miss Lillie is cutting up pineapples and bananas for the happy hour drinks and the subject of losing yourself and gifts one may pass up by not paying attention bring.

Once you lose yourself, you have two choices; find the person you used to be, or lose that person completely and change she explains. There are times in our life when we are given a "Gift" of some sort but we don't know it's a "Gift" at the time and we might pass it up, look at it weird or not even pay any attention at all. But what we really didn't see was the "Gift" we were given.

So in life remember, don't bypass anything because you never had it, felt it, or you feel it will interfere with your ego because it could be just what your life needs

Have a great day

Good Morning.

Meanwhile, down off the point in Gulf Shores at Tacky Jacks watching Susie a local artist carefully hand painting the sign that says "By land or by sea" the subject of stop worrying about your mistakes came up over baileys coffee.

Remember you don't owe anyone an explanation of your past, dwelling in the past stops you from moving towards your future, and anyone who judges you without knowing you is not part of YOUR future.

Life has its up's and downs but it's like the ocean, despite the storm, it's beautiful. What you go through today makes you stronger and makes you who you are, never ever stop believing in you

Have a great day.

Good Morning.

Meanwhile, down in San Antonio on the river walk where if you're not familiar with your surroundings can all seem like the rock paths that curve side to side following the small river are the same, there on the corner is Ruta Maya's coffee house.

The outside has handmade Mexican style umbrellas where you walk right up and sit down, Isabella will bring you coffee and say "Buenos días un día hermoso" Yes it is a beautiful morning. There the subject of deciding to live your life came up.

The best day of your life is the one on which you decide your life is your own. No apologies or excuses and no one to lean on, rely on, or blame. The gift is yours - it is an amazing journey - and you alone are responsible for the quality of it.

This is the day your life really begins.

Have an awesome day

Good Morning.

Meanwhile, down in Perdido Key,which is located on Florida's Panhandle as the southwestern-most part of Pensacola, FL. bordered on the west by Orange Beach, AL and the island that stretches about 15 miles east towards Santa Rosa Island.

There located at the corner of Sorrento Road and Gulf Beach Highway is Mojo's coffee shop where they have a featured frappe' called an "Almond Roca" that is a mixture of almond and cocoanut flavoring with Ghirardelli chocolate.

There you'll find "snowbirds", retiree's, local business folk, and vacationers shuffling in from the condos for a refreshing iced coffee or chai before heading out for more sun. This particular morning the subject of lessons learned came up and the people you meet really are for a reason along the way.

Life doesn't always introduce you to the people you WANT to meet. Sometimes life puts you in touch with the people you NEED to meet to help you, to hurt you, to leave you, to love you, and to gradually strengthen you into the person you were meant to become, live it love it and follow it but most importantly learn from it.

Have a great day.

Good Morning.

Meanwhile, back at La Boucherie Coffee House Located in the French quarter off of Chartres Street in New Orleans where the sounds of the night fade into the sounds of early morning and a different kind of people behind the scenes take over turning New Orleans into a culture only those who have experience it understand.

There having coffee watching people, he wondered why people do what they do?

My Dad who becomes wiser to me by the day, always told me "Son, two things you can't do run from your problems and borrow your way out of debt, very true words then and now.

Remember, what you run away from today, you will have to face tomorrow... stop running! Half the things we worry about never even happen, however your own mind is your biggest obstacle

Whatever you cannot change has changed you.

Have a great day

Good Morning.

Meanwhile, when growing up I spent most summers on family vacations to Myrtle Beach where golden beaches and family fun ruled the day.

My love of white sandy beaches came much later when I discovered the Gulf Coast. Also later I discovered right up from the now busy touristy Myrtle Beach about 8 miles up the coast to the sleepy non tourist town of Surf Side Beach, a more laid back community and much smaller enjoyable beach where serenity will find you.

There just off the main street pier is Jacob's Java Coffee House, where if you keep up with the sunrise time and if you set in the back corner booth you can experience the entire sunrise while sipping on your Coffee House Java with whipped cream.

Catalina, a girl from Holland who transferred here as an exchange student some years ago and never went home, and I one particular morning were discussing carving your own path for others to follow as she did when she decided to stay.

Do not go where the path may lead, go instead where there is no path and leave a trail. If you're trying to achieve, there will be roadblocks. I've had them; everybody has had them. But obstacles don't have to stop you.

If you run into a wall, don't turn around and give up. Figure out how to climb it, go through it, or work around it.

Have a great day

Good Morning.

Over the years in conversations in the places I've been I've taken down notes most of the time on napkins or whatever is available when someone say's something to reflect on.

Meanwhile down in St. Augustine Florida at Donovan's Irish Pub Affectionately known to the people who know as "Tess's place", named after Grandma Tess, another fine place that I love as I do most all Iris pubs along the way.

The subject of happiness come up and how it's true the more you live that the only thing that doesn't change is that everything changes, people scatter to the winds and constantly change their lives right in front of you.

Grandma Tess say's as we sip on Irish cream coffee, the only way to make sense out of change is to plunge into it, move with it, and join the dance Whoooooo Hoooooooo to change, She says.

Have a great day.

Good Morning.

 Meanwhile in Oklahoma City in the what the locals call the French Market Mall area, just a short walk from the famously haunted and mysterious Skirvin Hotel which is haunted by 'Effie' , a young maid who jumped to her death from the 10th floor in the 1930's and where the key to her room is proudly displayed on the wall in the hotel lobby. There you'll find Mojo's Blues Club, which is owed by a harmonica playing dentist called Dr. French E. Hickman or as the locals and I all call "Doc" there in the back close to the pool tables where the bar curves to the left the subject of directions and where you're headed came up.

Obstacles are only opportunities to succeed or fail; how we handle them determines what will happen. You can't change what you've started, but you can change the direction you are going. It's not what you are going to do, but it's what you're doing now that counts. Remember, if you're going down the wrong road. It's never too late to turn around.

Have a great day

Good Morning and Happy Monday

 Meanwhile, hidden down in Florida west of Laguna Beach and Santa Monica, and east of Riviera Beach but kept a quite secret unless you're looking for a condo is the sleepy Sunnyside Beach a place where you can escape away and enjoy the week.

There you'll find Rosetta's Place where early in the morning she's cutting up fresh fruit hand selected from Cocoa Island. There the subject of being real came up.

 Think about it! If you were ever really truly alone do you think you could have made it this far? Don't feel sorry for yourself and hate everything about life just because things may not be going your way! Do something about it! You're not helpless!

You may discover that in the long run you are much stronger than you believed and life will then take on a whole new meaning! Start living life, laugh, smile often, be a true friend. Pretending takes practice; being you comes natural so if your ass everyone will know it.

 Have a great day.

26

Good Morning!

It's interesting the people you meet along the way, the pretenders and the people going through changes in their life's and watching them face the things they never thought they would, and grow from it. Soon it will be warm and things will begin to change again, it's been a long cold winter but that's why we have the change of the seasons to keep moving on and appreciate what you haven't seen in a while.

The past is the past, its time! Got to get up and move on. Don't let your life slip through by living in the past or future. By living your life one day at a time, you live all the days of your life. It's a slippery road for dreamers and poets who fantasize of majestic places and deep-seated desires of the heart that their hands may never hold. The only dreams that are impossible are the ones you don't go after

Have a great day.

Good Morning!

Did you know spring is in 30 days? Better get those new flip flops
out ready to use. Have a great day and remember....Opportunity
does not knock; it presents itself when you beat down the damn
door, don't let anyone or anything stand in your way!

It's your life!!! What you do today can improve all your tomorrows
besides when your wildly successful it makes those entire nay
Sayers mad, you know the ones who always want to hold you down

Have a great day.

Good Morning!

Meanwhile, hidden down in Florida between Fort Myers Beach and Bonita Beach secretly held as a guarded secret, is Lovers Key.

For years, Lovers Key was accessible only by boat and it was said that only lovers traveled to the island to enjoy its remote and solitary beach. There, where the boats come in you'll find Angela whose grandparents discovered the island and where Walter proposed to his young bride to be over 60 years ago. Today you can still see the tree with their initials and date that captured the moment all those years ago. Angela can take you to the tree that still stands today like a monument to their long ago love affair.

There the discussion of right choices and the power of your own mind came up.

Your mind is the most powerful thing you possess, use it wisely or it will use you. Live life fully while you're here. Experience everything. Take care of yourself and your friends. Have fun, be crazy, and be weird. Go out and screw up! You're going to anyway, so you might as well enjoy the process. Take the opportunity to learn from your mistakes: find the cause of your problem and eliminate it. Don't try to be perfect; just be an excellent example of you.

Have a great day.

Good Morning.

 Meanwhile on the outskirts of Martha's Vineyard just a short walk down the way is the Dock St. Coffee Shop which occupies a tiny, narrow space between the bike rental on the corner and the Black Dog home wares store. What it lacks in size, it makes up for in quality.

 Every morning Rose walks down and gets a cup coffee. Ironically enough Rose sells roses by her flower stand next to the coffee shop, known as Rosie by the locals she wears her big white and yellow hats so everyone can see her, the hair in a long pony tail that reaches below her hips and tied with a purple ribbon. There this particular morning the subject of carving your own path and living by your rules came up.

Have you ever felt like that you're so afraid to hurt someone's feelings that you have a hard time saying NO? Even though you don't want to do something? well it's true the very first word we're taught is NO and for some reason becomes harder to say the older you get but here's the thing, you have to be honest with yourself first, stick to your plan, learn to say no more often, but more importantly if your plan does not go along with someone else's then by all means speak up, don't hesitate to be true to you.

If you don't design your own life plan, chances are you'll fall into someone else's plan. And guess what they have planned for you? Not much. Never give up!

 Have an awesome day

Good Morning!

Meanwhile, down on 2 Avenue F in Fort Pierce Florida situated on the banks of the Indian River is a place affectionately known as The Original Tiki Bar & Restaurant where the motto is "We overlook nothing . . . but the beautiful Indian River". There you'll find a picture of me taken with Janice Mintango that hangs near the right corner by the view of the river taken one afternoon after the bar opened back up in 2004 after the Treasure Coast of Florida was hit by two major hurricanes only weeks apart, Frances and Jeanne. Janice who came from Myrtle Beach to help the devastation of the coast from the hurricanes and feel in love with Fort Pierce and never left and I are discussing one particular morning the difference in dreaming and being a dreamer.

It's sometimes good to be a dreamer, as long as you have the ability to turn those dreams into reality. Getting caught in the imaginary world may provide temporary happiness, getting back to reality is what is important. Stick to your dreams, share them and make the most out of them. If you fear the future, there is none. If you look forward, there is one, so stop dreaming about and make it happen.

Have a great day

Good Morning!

Meanwhile, down on Honeymoon Island Florida close to Clearwater Florida is where you truly can get lost in a place that has sunshine on average 312 days a year. Honeymoon and neighboring Caladesi Island were originally it was part of a large barrier island that split in half during a major hurricane in 1921. The waterway between the islands is known as Hurricane Pass.

Caladesi Island is reachable by boat and ferry only from a dock on Honeymoon Island.

The story goes In the 1880s homesteader Henry Scharrer and his daughter Myrtle lived on the island. Later in life, at the age of 87, Myrtle Scharrer Betz penned the book, Yesteryear I Lived in Paradise, telling of her life of the barrier island, a must read if you have a beach, a hammock and time to waste away

Next to the ferry that seemingly takes you back in time to Caladesi Island is a small café, aptly named the Honeymoon Café located on the main beach. On most sunny mornings you can sit on a covered wooden deck facing the Gulf of Mexico and drink a cup of coffee in the time it takes the miniature ferry get larger as it reaches the shore where you are.

There the subject of negativity came up and the power that has over you. Take the weather, anytime you hear a 30% chance of rain people are all sad, I like to say that's 70% chance of sunshine, see the difference.

Remember today you'll only be as good as your ability to dismiss negative influences, practice points of wisdom, and unlock opportunities to release your happiness. Problems are 30% the issue and 70% how you respond to them don't worry when all you see is darkness. Behind the clouds there are always sunshine and blue skies. Have a great day!

Good Morning!

Meanwhile, looking down from The Upper Deck Coffee Shop down at The Tiki Bar the thought of the day is "Life and time." Success in life is a function of your willingness to accept change, one must adapt but never loose you're willingness to be you. Sometimes as much as some may not like it you can never be more than you. Every time you try to be something you're not or be something someone wants you to be you know you've pushed the time watch till you will get tired of it, sooner or later you will have to face the truth.

Remember, Yesterday has been washed away by the sea of time but today is pliable to our thoughts, today is moldable to our will, today will surely determine tomorrow. Choices, not Chances, are responsible for the quality of our Life.

Spend time to Think, Reflect, Introspect and then Choose

Have a great day.

Good Morning!

Meanwhile lost in a place where simple beauty seems to jump out at you at every turn and surrounded by the Great Smoky Mountains in scenic serenity and charm is the alluring Maggie Valley in North Carolina.

A place where as a kid we would take to the highway to a place called Ghost Town in the sky. Like a scene out of the movie Vacation or an old western it's an old amusement park where gun fighters take to the streets and the sheriff and his trusted deputies always win and the sound of the bell on the train can be heard from the chairlift that takes you up the mountain.

Over the years it turned into a real ghost town as the park was abandoned and seemed to be cursed by money problems.

For me in my mind it has always remained the same as it was when I had my picture taken there with my Dad.

Taking a ride up not too long ago on my Harley, a ride highly recommended just outside of Clyde, North Carolina you'll find The Coffee Cup Café where they pride themselves on a smile, cleanliness and southern charm.

There Charlotte named after another town in North Carolina will sit and share a cup of coffee.

One particular morning she and I were talking about following the road forward.

Sometimes in life it appears that we are at the end of our trail, when we're really at the beginning. If you take your direction from social signs, you'll just follow the herd and be programmed by other people who think for you, and are guided primarily by fear.

But if you follow your inspired inner voice of guidance, you'll be led to an experience that far surpasses any the sign-makers post.

Take to the highway and remember if you don't know where you're going any road will take you there

Have a great day

Good Morning.

Meanwhile on the side of Lookout Mountain situated half-way up past the famous Ruby Falls you'll find The Cravens House, originally built by Robert Cravens in 1838 and was a major point in the "Battle above the Clouds" during the Civil War. The house was destroyed during the war by drunken union soldiers during a brawl and was later rebuilt by Cravens.

If you take the right trail up the mountain and follow the sign markers to Point Park the trail makes the sounds of the busy city below as the cars rushing on their way, trains off in the distance blowing their horns and sirens screaming to their emergency disappear into the quietness of the trail.

A good morning hike will take you to the top where the awesome view of city below has many places to sit and reflect. The trail back is a short walk downhill past Point Park to the trail that leads to Sunset Rock and back down to The Cravens House. Sitting on Sunset Rock eating the packed lunch the subject of inner struggles came up.

The truth is that our finest moments are most likely to occur when we're feeling deeply uncomfortable, unhappy, or unfulfilled. For it is only in such moments, propelled by our discomfort, that we are likely to step out of our ruts and start searching for different ways or truer answers.

No matter how qualified or deserving we are, we'll never reach a better life until we can imagine it for ourselves and allow ourselves to have it.

All the wonders you seek are within yourself but always remember when dreaming of the future, don't let the present slip by

For my friends in Mobile who think I only write about the Gulf Have an awesome day.

Good Morning!

Meanwhile down in ST. Pete Beach, Florida hidden behind the popular Beachcomber Hotel there is a rustic treasure I love overlooking a private beach called JIMMY B's BEACH BAR.

Jimmy B's offers live entertainment day and night, seven days a week with an indoor and outdoor bar, a large bandstand, and a volleyball court. When the sun sets, they offer free Sunset Shooters to celebrate the occasion, the perfect place to watch the sun as it fades into the Gulf of Mexico.

The far right side opposite of the band are high top tables that lean back and aligns perfectly as the sun burns down at the end of the day glittering off the ocean. There the subject of respect came up over Sunset Shooters.

It's funny the longer you live the more you realize how important it is to have friendship.

If you've ever been in a relationship where YOU have no friends other than your mates then you're missing out on a very important part of you.

Once again a common theme here is it's your life, laughing, having fun with friends and smiling every day is so important to your future, health and happiness.

Moving on, gives you a chance to explore yourself and to fall in love with yourself again, which I highly recommend. We generally love to sort out the truth from mysterious things, but do we sort out the truth of life? This in itself is a mystery.

You must take personal responsibility. You cannot change the circumstances, the seasons, or the wind, but you can change yourself and therefor your future.

Remember, Losers live in the past. Winners learn from the past and enjoy working in the present toward the future

Have a great day.

Good Morning!

Meanwhile, my love of lighthouses has taken me on many adventures to places I would've never seen without them this is one discovery.

 Seemingly lost but never forgotten, twisted and turned, reshaped and reformed by hurricanes and Confederate soldiers, Spanish explorers long ago and often rediscovered as it was originally In 1519, by the Spanish explorer Alonzo Pineda who was the first documented European to visit, staying long enough to map the island with remarkable accuracy is Dauphine Island.

The Gulf of Mexico is to the south of the island; the Mississippi Sound and Mobile Bay are to the north. The island's eastern end helps to define the mouth of Mobile Bay. The eastern, wider portion of the island is shaded by thick stands of pine trees, but the narrow, western part of the island features scrub growth and few trees.

So the legend goes The Island's French history began on January 31, 1699, when the explorer Pierre Le Moyne, sieur d'Iberville, one of the founders of French Louisiana, arrived at Mobile Bay, and anchored near the island on his way to explore the mouth of the Mississippi River. D'Iberville named it "Isle Du Massacre" (Massacre Island) because of a large pile of human skeletons discovered there. The gruesome site turned out to be a simple burial mound which had been broken open by a hurricane, not a massacre site, but the name stuck. Fort Gaines on the eastern tip of the island was built between 1821 and 1848. It was occupied by Confederate forces in 1861, and captured by Federal troops during the Battle of Mobile Bay. The phrase, "Damn the torpedoes, full speed ahead," was spoken by U. S. Admiral David Farragut just a few hundred yards from Dauphin Island's shore.

If you make it that far down to this remote Island you'll surly be welcomed at the Lighthouse Bakery by Christa who is the daughter of the owners.

This place is like going to your grandparent's house as a kid where everything is fresh baked, the smell pulls you off the road.

There over coffee watching the seagulls and roosters graze together just off the shore the subject of happiness with conditions came up.

Most people ask for happiness on condition, but long-term happiness can only be felt if you don't set conditions. Accept life unconditionally. Realize that life balances itself between the ideal and the disappointing.

Remember this and say it often, the disappointments are just life's way of saying, "I've got something better for you right around the corner." So be patient, live life, today is the tomorrow you spoke about yesterday now the time has come to live it.

Have a great day.

Good Morning.

Today is a brand new day a fresh start. Replace negativity with positivity. Think happy thoughts. Inspire yourself. Create. Laugh, play, love and learn.

Give someone a compliment. Perform a random act of kindness. Take a chance on an idea you believe in. You have the opportunity to do these things every single day to make the necessary changes and slowly become the person you want to be.

You just have to decide to do it. Decide that today is the day. Say it: "This is going to be my day!"

Good Morning!

Meanwhile, down at The Sandbar Sports Grill in Cocoa Beach which is known for great drinks like the Hurricane, awesome food and live music all the time, where the catch phrase is We don't run from Hurricanes... we drink um!

Darleen is getting ready for the day by selecting fresh fruit to slice up brought in by Oscar, a local farmer. There the subject of making you a priority came up.

Truth be told, there are only a few people in this world who will stay 100% true to you, and YOU should be one of them don't you think? Don't sit back and let things happen to you. Go out and happen to things. You are what you do, not what you say you'll do. Stop saying "I wish" and start saying "I will." Turn your cant's into cans and your dreams into plans. Don't you think it's about time to get your head out of your ass and start being happy?

Go out and have an awesome day and be true to you and remember there are two kinds of pain: pain that hurts and pain that changes you. But when you accept life, instead of resisting it, both kinds help you grow.

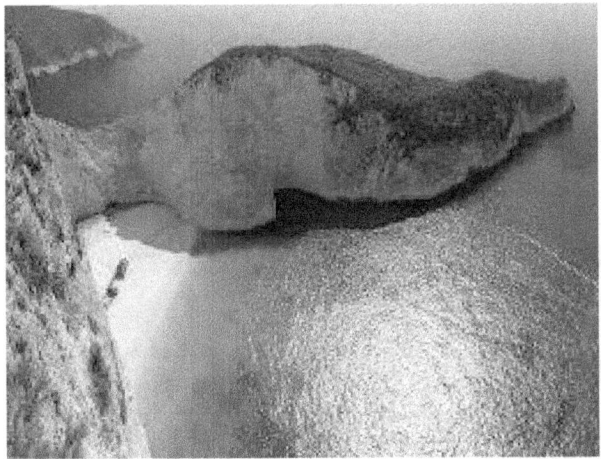

Good Morning Happy Tuesday

Meanwhile, down on Anna Maria Island approximately seven miles long north to south and worlds away from popular neighboring Siesta Key, the white sands of Anna Maria are peaceful and relaxing and not for people-watching.

There are no volleyball nets or parasail boats in sight and the plane that flies over touristy beaches pulling the daily special never comes here, happy hour is any hour you spend here. And that's just the way its proponents like it. Just pack a small cooler, bring a beach read and plant yourself on its white sandy beach.

Anna Maria Island, sometimes called Anna Maria Key, is a barrier island on the coast of Manatee County, Florida bounded on the west by the Gulf of Mexico, on the south by Longboat Pass (which separates it from Longboat Key), on the east by Anna Maria Sound, and on the north by Tampa Bay.

Ponce de Leon was said to have named the island for Maria Anna von der Pfalz-Neuburg, the queen of Charles II of Spain, the sponsor of his expedition to explore the islands.

Anna Maria Island is served by a free trolley-style bus that runs north and south on Gulf Drive and starts every morning at Anna Maria Island Beach Cafe located Where Manatee Avenue Meets the Gulf.

There one morning sipping on a Tropical Papaya Batido which is A sunlit, vitamin-packed tropical fruit shake made with pink-hued papayas, fresh squeezed oranges and bananas Yum Yum! The subject of spending time with the wrong people came up.

Life is too short to spend time with people who suck the happiness out of you. If someone wants you in their life, they'll make room for you. You shouldn't have to fight for a spot. Never, ever insist yourself to someone who continuously overlooks your worth.

Remember, it's not the people that stand by your side when you're at your best, but the ones who stand beside you when you're at your worst that are your true friends.

Have a great day

Some of the most beautiful sunsets you'll ever see are here on

Anna Maria Island

The Tiki Man.

Good Morning!

There are many places in the south where charm and beauty collide creating breathtaking views of sunsets and sunrises, where the promise of a new day brings new adventures and new beginnings.

One particular island located on the shores of Georgia where none more charming places can be found then nearby sweet Savannah where the Savannah River empties into the Atlantic Ocean you'll find Tybee Island.

The island is the northeastern-most of Georgia's Barrier Islands, which comprise the outer section of the state's Lower Coastal Plain region. Like the other Barrier Islands, Tybee consists of a sandy beach on its eastern shore and a tidal salt marsh on its western shore. Once called "Savannah Beach" in the 1950's and as recent as the 1970's Tybee" is the Native American Indian tribe Euchee word for "salt".

There laying in the sun with her long black hair in the wind, shades on and a much needed time long overdue is Kristy, with the warm sun on her face watching her little ones play in the sand and wonders how long the peacefulness of her day will last. An amazing woman with a heart of gold often left to pick up pieces and seemingly make something out of nothing she prides herself on the desire and will to survive and does it but often secretly wishes things were different if only for a day like this one.

There the subject of lessons learned came up.

I suppose we all wish we could jump in the time machine and set the date to a certain place in the past such as the day you turned 18. All the things you would love to tell yourself if you could travel back in time to give your 18-year-old self some advice about life hmmm.

I guess I would tell my 18-year-old self to commit myself to making lots of mistakes. Mistakes teach you important lessons.

The biggest mistake you can make is doing nothing because you're too scared to make a mistake. So don't hesitate – don't doubt yourself. In life, it's rarely about getting a chance; it's about taking a chance.

You'll never be 100% sure it will work, but you can always be 100% sure doing nothing won't work.

Most of the time you just have to go for it! And no matter how it turns out, it always ends up just the way it should be. Either you succeed or you learn something a "Win-Win".

Remember, if you never act, you will never know for sure, and you will be left standing in the same spot forever. But above all, laugh when you can, apologize when you should, and let go of what you can't change.

Life is short, yet amazing. Enjoy the ride Have a great day everyone

For Kristy, thanks for the summer 2012

Good Morning!

Spring is often described as a new beginning with a promise of a new season.

Where we live, people in Harrison Bay the first sign of spring is normally birds outside your window waking you up. Shortly after that the Bradford Pear Tress begins to bloom and dogwoods shortly after that.

This time of the year I cut the ceiling fan on in The Tiki Bar because there is a certain bird who returns every year to try and nest there.

Springing forward is what it really is and not just the season. Let today be the day you stop being haunted by the ghosts from your past. What happened in the past is just one chapter in your story; don't close the book, just turn the page.

We've all been hurt by our own decisions and by others, and while the pain of these experiences is normal, sometimes it lingers for too long. Feelings of resentment urge us to relive the same pain over and over, and we have a hard time letting go.

Forgiveness is the remedy. It allows you to focus on the future without combating the past.

To understand the infinite potential of everything going forward is to forgive everything already behind you. Without forgiveness, wounds can never be healed and personal growth can never be achieved. It doesn't mean you're erasing the past, or forgetting what happened. It means you're letting go of the resentment and pain, and instead choosing to learn from the incident and move on with your life.

So today spring will finally be here so spring forward and the leave the past behind

Have a great day. *For my son Jeffery who was born in the spring.*

Good Morning!

Most people who know me would probably say I'm the one person in the room if asked my opinion will tell you. I've never been much for being the YES guy which by the way has brought me much success in business over the years and just as many headaches ☺

I was in a meeting a couple of weeks ago where we have a new leader in our company and I was conducted the meeting and the topic of customer complaints came up.

Once used quite often where if you make one customer mad you make 10 others mad because the people go tell 10 others and it grows from there.

I had to disagree with this analogy or as I put it take it a step further, now because I believe we're way past that. I got to tell you and make sure you use this in your next meeting or presentation.

Today in the world we're living in you're only one Facebook post or Twitter post away from being the worst place in town, so be careful how you handle that next issue.

With that said you're also one post away from being the worst husband, wife, boyfriend, girlfriend, neighbor or friend as well. Now most people would also say I'm the guy who hates drama, I suppose it comes from a personal decision I made to be happy a quest really.

Living your life for you and being a good friend, neighbor or family member is really a choice we all make and I choose to be happy, makes life so much more fun.

A big part of who you become in life has to do with who you choose to surround yourself with. Sometimes luck controls who walks into your life, but you decide who you let stay, who you pursue, and who you let walk back out. Ultimately, you should surround yourself with people who make you a better person and let go of those who don't.

 Have a great day!

I choose to me that day and moving forward.

Good Morning!

Meanwhile located between Panama City Beach and Destin Florida is one of the most unique towns along the beach you'll find.

Known for its film debut, The Truman Show, Seaside, Florida is a classic beach town complete with white picket fences, pastel-colored houses, and clear blue Gulf waters.

If you saw the movie then you probably thought the perfect little town was made on a Hollywood movie set but no it's real.

There just as in the movie you'll find the Seaside coffee shop or better known as Amavida's seaside coffee and tea complete with white picket fences and ocean view. Just a short stroll on the sugar white sand away in the evening local guitarist will play the sounds of the islands to make you feel at home.

Early in the morning you can check out the daily special on the chalk board out front that Carissa writes with her own style of imagination.

Capturing her attention one morning her and I was discussing things you should stop doing to yourself.

The most painful thing is losing yourself in the process of loving someone too much, and forgetting that you are special too.

Yes, help others; but help yourself too. If there was ever a moment to follow your passion and do something that matters to you, that moment is now.

One of the greatest challenges in life is being yourself in a world that's trying to make you like everyone else.

Someone will always be prettier, someone will always be smarter, someone will always be younger, but they will never be you.

Don't change so people will like you. Be yourself and the right people will love the real you.

Remember get busy living or get busy dying is not just a line from a movie. You can't start the next chapter of your life if you keep *rereading* your last one

Have a great day. *For Kimberly M.*

Good Morning.

Meanwhile, did you know there are undeveloped beaches in Florida that hurricanes love? It's true really there are a lot of them where no one but those that do know go or stubble across them by accident.

There's one particular, Navarre Beach where hurricanes love to go such as Erin and Opal in 1995, Hurricane Ivan in September 2004, and Hurricane Dennis in July 2005 each had significant impacts on the beach.

Land falling hurricanes cause significant damage due to its position on a low-lying barrier island. Other hurricanes were Hurricane Katrina in 2005, Hurricane Gustav in 2008, and Hurricane Isaac in 2012.

It's also where much of the 1978 film Jaws 2 was filmed. Hotel scenes in the movie were filmed at the Navarre Beach Holiday Inn where it was destroyed by Hurricane Ivan. Oh the love the hurricanes have for this beach is a long history.

The cool thing about that is each time one hits it changes it just a bit, if it's been a while since you've been there you can tell the changes right away. When this happens its God's way of rewarding the beach by replacing its sugar white sands with new even more white sand out of the gulf, in return the beach gets to stand alone to be itself a sparkling wonder of endurance

This reminds me a lot of us when things do go wrong.

In time, changes are bound to happen to us but there is always a reward after the storm, you just have to be able to see them.

Remember, In the end, loving your life is about trusting your intuition, taking chances, losing and finding happiness, cherishing the memories, and learning through experience. It's a long-term journey.

You have to stop worrying, wondering, and doubting every step of the way. Laugh at the confusion, live consciously in the moment, and enjoy your life as it unfolds.

You might not end up exactly where you intended to go, but you will eventually arrive precisely where you need to be.

Have a great day.

Good Morning!

Meanwhile, on the west side of the island of Puerto Rico where some of the world's best surfing beaches including Domes, Marias, Tres Palmas, Sandy Beach, Pools Beach and home to Caribbean beaches including Córcega Beach can be found, you'll find the town and beaches of Rincón.

Where if you like coffee as I do, then I highly recommend you bring your own coffee as Puerto ricin coffee is as thick as syrup, next watch out for the lizards.

Most of the remote places you stay in on the far side of the island far away from the glamor and tourist in San Juan have screens not windows and if they are windows they're small and crank up and down. The kitchens can be found on the back porch overlooking breathtaking beaches and true Caribbean feel, there is where you cook breakfast where an occasional lizard may startle you from time to time.

If you go make sure you take time to visit the small towns made of rock and brick roads where the tropical rainforest in El Yunque is a must see, just make sure to bring a poncho it rains everyday there. If you like Rum producing it has long been an important part of Puerto Rico's economy since the 16th century. Make sure to pick up a bottle of Don Q before finding your way to the beach

There From your seat at the Lazy Parrot poolside bar, you can watch as Pizza Chef Gaby Carrero creates his gourmet pizzas using fresh dough and homemade marinara sauce cooked in specially designed Italian brick ovens with Gaby's touch.

One morning sitting at the Lazy Parrot watching Gaby roll the balls of dough for the day, the subject of the moment you start listening to your inner voice, rather than defying it came up.

Sometimes your mind needs more time to accept what your heart already knows. So take some time to breathe. Be a witness, not a judge. Listen to your intuition.

How many times have you said later "I should have went with my gut" or the one I hear a lot "I knew it" that one always makes me laugh I normally say, well if you knew it why didn't tell someone like the two people that needs to know the most YOU and ME!

Remember, every ending is the beginning of something else. Every exit is an entry somewhere else.

As long as you are breathing, it's never too late; every day is a new opportunity.

Today is one of the good ole days you're going to miss someday.

Live today without regrets, hate and fear of the unknown.

Have a great day.

Good Morning.

There's line I like from a Jimmy Buffett song "we only sail in circles on this crazy round ball, sometimes we get dizzy but we can never really truly fall off".

I like the think our lives are one giant circle with four sides and are constantly in motion. In order for it to be always rotating forward, none of the four sides can be compromised.

The four sides are kindness to others at all times, humility in all areas of life, being grateful for everything and everyone your life touches, and happiness in every facet of your life.

Without these four corners of your life's circle being part of your everyday life, your circle of motion will be stopped, so always sail forward when the shore you left behind comes back around and it will, you'll be a much stronger sailor

Have an awesome day.

Good Morning.

Let's drift on down to the beach shall we?

Take a walk down early in the morning finding that spot on the beach where you will live for the day, smell of sun tan lotion on the breeze, the sound of the waves crashing creeping their way up the white sugar sand, the distant sound of the wave riders setting up for the day, the early sounds of a distant guitar playing a tropical tune.

At the end of the Cocoa Beach Pier you'll find the fantastic Mai Tiki Bar 800 feet out over the water where their saying is "NO BAR GOES THIS FAR"

There one sunny morning the subject of rewards of life came up.

For everything you win, you lose something so the reward of what you think is a win must be an important one.

Life is a song sing it. Life is a game play it. Life is a challenge meet it. Life is a dream realize it. Life is a sacrifice offer it. Life is love - enjoy it.

In three words I can sum up everything I've learned about life: it goes on.

Life is a series of natural and spontaneous changes.

Don't resist them that only leads to sorrow let reality be reality. Let things flow naturally forward in whatever way they like.

Have a great day.

Your inner voice knows the way.....listen.

Good Morning.

Meanwhile, down on the many Islands of South Carolina where getting lost is a good thing and the trip never planned can easily become the best trip.

There you'll find none other better place to get lost on then the Sea Island Parkway.

There following your sense of adventure you'll find Harbor Island, a small resort island located 14 miles east of Beaufort, South Carolina. It's one of the Carolina's many Sea Islands.

The majority of the island is tidal marsh; a swing drawbridge carry crossing the Harbor River connects the island to St. Helena Island towards the west. A small causeway crossing Johnson Creek connects Harbor Island with Hunting Island towards the south.

Nestled amidst majestic oaks is the Harbor Town Bakery & Café truly known around the island for great home-cooked breakfasts, soups, salads, Panini's and pastries, and everything is baked fresh daily.

There next door to the bakery you'll find Maggie, who came to the Islands from New Orleans with the dream of owning a simple bait shop in a small cozy town far away from the drama of work, family and past life filled with constantly putting her dream on hold.

Maggie whose hair is long and curly whose sassy personality fits right in with the local fisherman and occasional tourist seeking and following their own dreams.

There with her love of coffee and the morning sunrise the subject of slowing down came up as the sun peaks through the boats gently rocking on the morning waves.

Sometimes it's okay if the only thing you're doing is breathing. Life can get so crazy, tough and complicated, but always take the time to slow down, calm down, reflect, and appreciate what you have and NOT, what you don't have.

There is always someone out there who wishes they had what you have right now. You show me a man who has everything and I'll show you a man who wants more!

You just have to be happy being you and living in the moment. Remember, Just because someone doesn't want to be with you doesn't mean you're not special; it just means they're not the right kind of special for you,

Your past is your best teacher for your future

Have an awesome day and slow down and get lost on your on island roads.

For Maggie who dreamed of a bait shop.

Good Morning.

Today's forecast is slightly salty with a hint of lime, ocean breeze will slightly and warm move in from the south

Today's message is simple

There is only one way to happiness and that is to cease worrying about things which are beyond the power of our will.

Let it go and what is supposed to be and it will be.

Remember while you're worrying about all the things you can't change or want, happiness often sneaks in through a door you didn't know you left open

Have a great day.

Good Morning.

Meanwhile traveling down to the Gulf is truly one of my favorite places to be.

Of all the places I've been the white sand off the Gulf of Mexico is a home away from home and holds a special place in my heart.

My love of Tiki Bars was discovered there and idea of building my on Tiki Bar in Harrison Bay came from Gulf Shores after a week there by alone many years ago.

You could be spending time at The Hangout or sipping on a Bushwacker at The Bama or better known as Flora-Bama where before its partial destruction by Hurricane Ivan in 2004, it boasted in the range of 20 bars on the grounds. In addition, up to 4 live bands could be playing simultaneously providing a wide array of music for visitors to enjoy.

The Jimmy Buffett song "Bama Breeze" was written about this roadhouse that was original built in 1964. I don't believe you could truly call yourself a Parrot Head which I'm proud to say I am if you haven't spent time at "The Bama"

What is a Parrot Head?

The term Parrot Head first came into fruition when Jimmy Buffett was performing at Timberwolf Amphitheatre at Kings Island in Ohio, just outside of Cincinnati.

Jimmy commented on all those crazy folks in the crowd who were wearing tropical Hawaiian shirts and parrot hats and who keep coming back to every show and went from there.

Anyway I don't believe you can call yourself one if you've never been to Jimmy Buffett's Sisters place Lucy's in Gulf Shores better known as Lulu's.

Lulu's is one of the finest jewels of LA (Lower Alabama). Nestled peacefully on the intercostal waterway, Lulu's at Homeport is girded by its own unique marina complete with coastal whimsy and charm, a one-of-a-kind atmosphere.

There is where I also discovered the band The Boat Drunks who sings one of my favorite songs "Long Time No Sea"

One afternoon at Lulu's the subject of things you should stop doing to YOU came up.

Stop complaining and feeling sorry for you is a good topic these days.

You know life's curveballs are thrown for a reason to shift your path in a direction that is meant for you. You may not see or understand everything the moment it happens, and it may be tough. But reflect back on those negative curveballs thrown at you in the past. You'll often see that eventually they led you to a better place, person, state of mind, or situation. So smile!

Let everyone know that today you are a lot stronger than you were yesterday, and you will be.

Have an awesome Friday and a fantastic weekend and pay no attention to the spring showers passing by, it's just Mother Nature watering the flowers.

Good Morning.

 Meanwhile, back at the beach The Long Island Tiki Bar is beginning to get ready for the lunch crowd and the music is playing island sounds and makes you feel right at home.

The ocean breeze feels warm on your face and the bright colors of the umbrellas put up by Sandy early in the morning look as if they're painted in the picture you're gazing at, as a plane flies over with Happy Hour specials at various places along the beach.

 From The Tiki Bar the smells enlighten your senses of coconut, strawberries, bananas, mangoes and oranges.

Today will be a good day if you make the good out of today.

 From a travelers point of view I've often thought life is one big road with lots of signs.

So when you're riding through the ruts, don't complicate your mind. Flee from hate, mischief and jealousy. Don't bury your thoughts but put your vision to reality. Wake Up and Live! Go after what you want, but if you choose not to, don't be sad when someone else has what you wanted, there's really is no one to blame.

Tip of the day, the thing that is really hard, and really amazing, is giving up on being perfect and beginning the work of becoming yourself. Smile you're amazing

Have a great day.

Good Morning.

Meanwhile, the song Changes In Latitudes, Changes In Attitudes where Jimmy takes off for a weekend to reflect always reminds me of The Coconut Hideaway located on Little Gasparilla island, part of the Gulf Island chain that includes Sanibel, Captiva and Boca Grande.

Another secret hideaway and very special island which offers something those other tourist islands cannot…privacy and seclusion.

This bridgeless barrier island just 10 minutes from the mainland and just north of Boca Grande has no roads and no traffic, just white sandy paths for exploring. There you'll find yourself surrounded by the way Florida used to be before condos and high rises took over the powder white sands.

So the story goes as I was told Gasparilla Island gets its name from the legendary pirate captain José Gaspar "Gasparilla", who had his base on the island and purportedly hid his fabulous treasure there sometime in the 1800's and has never been found.

They are many legendary stories of the captain but none more than the ending after a battle with the pirate hunting schooner USS Enterprise.

In the battle that followed Gasparilla's ship was riddled by cannon balls. Rather than surrender, Gaspar chained the anchor around his waist and leapt from the bow, shouting "Gasparilla dies by his own hand, not the enemy's and so the legend began.

Back at The Coconut Hideaway one morning after hearing the demise of Captain Gasper the subject of never giving up was discussed by the beautiful Mesmerella and me.

Don't be afraid to get back up and to try again, to love again, to live again, and to dream again. Don't let a hard lesson harden your heart. Life's best lessons are often learned at the worst times and from the worst mistakes. There will be times when it seems like everything that could possibly go wrong is going wrong. And you might feel like you'll be stuck in this rut forever, but you won't.

When you feel like quitting, remember that sometimes things have to go very wrong before they can be right. Sometimes you have to go through the worst, to arrive at your best

Have an awesome day and if you ever make it to Gasparilla island don't look for the treasure just find yourself.

You are the treasure.

Good Morning Happy Thursday

 Got a call from a girl the other day who once worked for me years ago and who calls me from time to time.

 Once a very confused employee and with a little help and advice she now manages a top company and considers me her mentor, to use her words.

It's important to have mentors in your professional life as they often affect your personal life as well. She says she uses my #1 rule all the time and begins to tell me a story and we both laughed of the outcome and how it always works for her.

My #1 rule has always been that its ok to disagree but it's never ok to become disagreeable, meaning that once we listen to each other's concerns as a team when we get up and go back to work we're both on the same page, one team working towards the same goal.

We may not always agree on a way forward but we all must move in the right direction.

Through the years, the tears, the smiles and the miles I've learned that you can teach anyone to be a quitter or you can teach people to NEVER quit! , the second part will get you much further down the road in business and life in general. I don't believe you have to be better than everybody else. I believe you have to be better than you ever thought you could be.

 Have a great day.

Good Morning.

Life is an adventure, live every day to the fullest. Hold onto the good times and let all the bad times fall behind you

Understand that life is precious and so very short. Each of us should wake up and be happy to be alive and breathing, thank God that the coffee pot is still working and another day of opportunity has come our way if for only a day.

Smile, it is contagious.

Have a great day.

Good Morning.

Meanwhile, I had an opportunity one time to travel to one of quietest barrier islands on the Gulf Coast located south from my beloved Anna Maria Island, between Sarasota Bay and the Gulf of Mexico.

Its history includes tales of explorers and Native Americans, pirates and pioneers. There are grand mansions and even grander yachts, plus some of the world's most beautiful sunsets lining the beauty of the Gulf of Mexico. There is Longboat Key.

Known for tasteful luxury and manicured surroundings, Longboat Key is rich in gorgeous beaches and of course beautiful sunsets. If you go spend a few hours off of the Gulf of Mexico on the deck of the Lazy Lobster.

There you'll find Ava who came from Australia to go to school there and fell in love with the Gulf as most people do. There the subject of forgiveness came up as she talked about how she never really lived up to others in her life and how she woke up one day and realized THIS IS MY LIFE!!

One thing for sure you can't change mistakes made with people in the past, but you can change the outcome of those mistakes at any time by taking responsibility for them. Do what is right to best correct those mistakes ofd the past and accept them so that you can be forgiven and forgive yourself.

Most people usually have already forgiven you they're just waiting for you to forgive yourself so that you can both move on.

Don't set your eyes on the past. Don't focus your thoughts on past achievement achieve more. Take your mind off the hurt and pain of the past.

Whenever you want to look back, remember today is tomorrows future, what will you make of it now?

Have a great day and just be you.

Good morning

I read a story one time about two twin sisters that we're separated by each other as children after a horrible accident where they lost both parents. They spent most of their life's searching for each other and accidently bumped into one another in a hospital in California after being in an accident where THEY crashed into each other, they we're born in Florida.

This was proof positive that all things happen for a reason.

Sometimes when you're looking or searching for something it usually comes along when you least expect it. Each choice we make causes a ripple effect in our lives. When things happen to us, it is the reaction we choose that can create the difference between the sorrow of our past and the happiness in our future. Just like the story of the two sisters every choice they made brought them together.

Remember, opportunities are like sunrises. If you wait too long, you miss them.

Have a great day.

Good Morning.

Meanwhile, taking a walk down by the boardwalks of beaches and places along the coast early in the morning is a favorite pastime of mine when the opportunity comes up. Early morning time to reflect and choose directions to go is needed. Some people meditate, some fly by the seat of their pants and some like me make it up as they go BUT I do spend time thinking of directions, I'm just not that eager to make a mistake as some.

Still I think that every day you waste doing something or being something you don't want to be or involved in something you know is not good for you whether a friendship or relationship is the worst thing one can do to one's self, there is only one today. The past is a bucket of ashes, so live not in your yesterdays, not just for tomorrow, but in the here and now. Keep moving and forget the past mortems.

Remember, no one can get the jump on the future but decisions you make today may very well create the future both good and bad.

You may have a fresh start any moment you choose, Said the mermaid fortuneteller to the wise Tiki Man, for this thing that we call 'failure' is not the falling down, but the staying down.

Have a great day.

Good Morning.

Meanwhile, down in Seaside where the color of white represents clean and happiness and yellow reminds you of the bright umbrella's and sailboat sails that go by on a lazy day. The boardwalks crisscross back and forth on their way to the sea. There sits Kimberly a girl with a beautiful smile who knows she has built fences around her heart. She knows that if she spent more time on her own happiness then, well she would be.

She thinks of the man she would love to get to know more but always puts herself last, just one more day she thinks.

What about you? Been doing some rewinding, regrouping, rethinking and cutting ties have you?

You know finishing projects and reshaping your world to what you want it to be can be difficult at times. Take relationships, you've finally made up your mind to move on and some junk mail comes in the mail that has your ex's name on it and you want to blow up the mail box, Its all ok and just part of it.

Placing ourselves as number one is unselfish, if what we are aiming for betters our life, health, relationships and existence.

To have a vision, does not mean that everyone needs to be onboard with it. If it is in your heart, follow your heart.

Time spent alone, to listen to the inner voice in keeping your compass pointing in your own direction, also roots a deep friendship with yourself the one who can support you the most.

Free yourself of the ties that prevent you from being you, take a chance a leap of faith.

Remember when opportunity knocks stop asking "Who is it?" Just open the door, you know

Have a great day.

She knew this girl on the beach where she wanted to be.

Good Morning

Words of wisdom scribbled on napkin from The Tiki Bar for today is, nothing can truly hold us back from becoming who we want to be we choose our fate, and every excuse is just another nail in the coffin.

 Instead of focusing on the reasons of 'why not' to do something, we need to just get up and take responsibility for our lives and live them the way we would want to remember them.

Remember we don't have memories sometimes they have you.

Have a great day

Good Morning

Meanwhile, taking a break from hanging hats in Joyce's flip flop shop in Laguna Beach, Florida on a sunny Tuesday spring morning, Joyce ask if I would like a Raspberry Corona Cocktail smoothie? hmmmm why yes I would. Her daughter Sabrina comes in from the local fruit market in Seaside wearing one of her mom's handmade hats made of all colors that remind you of the beach.

She's been collecting fruit for the afternoon happy hour drinks at the Great Southern Cafe and said she would make them. Both Sabrina and Her mom have long blond hair that flows past their waste and winning smiles that make the whole shop bright and inviting.

Sabrina worked at a local sea turtle hospital when she was going through business school which I find interesting for my friend Jennifer back home. There over the smoothies the discussion of determination came up with Sabrina and me.

One of my things I do not like are lazy people, I truly believe laziness is not taught but acquired by those who always want to take the easy way out of things either responsibility, work ethic or just taking care of what you have. I believe in working hard and playing hard but always taking time for family and deserving friends in the here and now.

Now is more important than tomorrow. Yes I plan for the future and tend to always think a little further down the road then most of the people I know BUT what's most important is today.

Remember to set your sights high, the higher the better. Expect the most wonderful things to happen, not in the future but right now. Realize that nothing is too good. Allow absolutely nothing to hamper you or hold you up in any way.

With that said I've also learned that luck is quite predictable. If you want more luck, take more chances. Be more active. Show up more often. As I often say today is the tomorrow you talked about yesterday

Have an awesome day.

Good Morning

Meanwhile, Twelve miles northwest of Chestertown, Maryland up the eastern coast hidden away from the popular and busy Ocean City is where you'll find "The Jewel of the Chesapeake." or better known as Betterton Beach.

Dating back to the Seventeenth century it was a major fishing port for 100 years until the great depression.

With its Victorian-style homes, a few sprawling rooming houses, and tiny summer cottages it gives you a glimpse of days gone by. If you're looking for a secret beach or a place to hide away up the coast this is it.

There located off of Ericsson Ave looking out at the distant and mysteries ocean as if to see ghost ships from the past arriving you'll find the Sunset Beach Bar And Grill. There looking out at the waters and the pier the subject of blaming others came up over coffee.

When you stop blaming others for your troubles then and only then can you begin to move in the right direction, the extent to which you can achieve your dreams depends on the extent to which you take responsibility for your life.

When you blame others for what you're going through, you deny responsibility and you give others power over that part of your life. This often leads to worry and Worry will not strip tomorrow of its burdens, it will strip today of its smiles.

One way to check if something is worth mulling over is to ask yourself this one question: "Will this matter in one year's time? Three years? Five years?" If not, then it's not worth worrying about. Move on take responsibility, say "I was wrong" and go on down the road and smile. Have a great day.

Remember Positive action to make the future better is the best solution to forget negative results of the past! Choose to make a difference in your life! Always stay a strong encourager and guide others to do the same!

Do it every day and DO IT BIG!!!"

Good Morning.

Meanwhile, stories of places and people, pirates and treasures, sandy beaches and sunsets far away are dear to my heart. One such place wrapped in Hurricanes and Pirate legends with history from another time and place is straight down US 1 towards the Florida Keys.

There you'll find Upper Matecumbe Key where the legend of the 1733 Spanish Galleon Capitana will lure you into her mystery. She carried more than two thousand boxes of gold and silver coins and bullion, hundreds of ingots of copper, as well as cochineal, indigo, vanilla, chocolate, and tobacco. Also known as El Rubi she was the flagship of the 1733 fleet, carrying the king's treasure.

During a hurricane the Capitana grounded just inside the reef line northeast of Upper Matecumbe Key. She had been leaking badly before she ran aground and no one aboard was expected to survive. She lay there till she was rediscovered in modern times in 1938.

Upper Matecumbe Key has a history of family's homesteading hundreds of acres only to give into the raging hurricanes throughout history. Walking around you can see these makers from long ago. The island traps the treasure and the dreams of the people that came before and after and keeps reinventing herself.

 Reminds me of the changes we all go through, how chapters of our life define you as you go.

I like to think chapters of your life are 5 years at a time.

Think about it, where we're you 5 years ago? 10 years ago? And so on. Every chapter defines you a little more.... The thing that matters is the chapter you're in, that's most important. If one tries to relive chapters you may find yourself living in the past and losing sight of your future. Be careful of your thoughts, sometimes it's not the pain that makes you suffer; it's your own negative thoughts that make things seem worse. Is it really?

At some point quality of life becomes more important. The quality of our life purely depends on the type of thoughts we entertain in our minds. Our inner thoughts create our outer world.

No matter how qualified or deserving you are, you will never reach a better life until you can imagine it for yourself and allow yourself to have it.

Remember, Life doesn't really have to be about live and learn if were willing to learn to live

Have an awesome day.

Good Morning

It's a brand new day might as well get up and make the most of it.

Thought of the day from The Tiki Bar

How about stop berating yourself for old mistakes?

We may love the wrong person and cry about the wrong things, but no matter how things go wrong, one thing is for sure, mistakes help us find the person and things that are right for us.

We all make mistakes, have struggles, and even regret things in our past. But you are not your mistakes, you are not your struggles, and you are here NOW with the power to shape your day and your future. Every single thing that has ever happened in your life is preparing you for a moment that is yet to come.

Remember good things come to those who get off their ass and make it happen

Have a great day.

Good Morning!

 Meanwhile, driving down highway 10 towards Florida across the mobile bay bridge between Mobile and Daphne is a place called Spanish Fort. Spanish Fort is rich in history dating as far back as 1712. This is originally the site of a trading post established by French-occupied Mobile.

Take the exit where you see the USS Alabama and go left under the bridge. Heading down this road you will occasionally be stopped by a crossing alligator on its way to the other side. Driving further out past the popular Oyster House is place I use to call home called The Bluegill Restaurant.

Parking out by the big Bluegill sign by the road, you stroll across the gravel drive and up the wooden stairs. This is more of my type of place to hang out, with its character and history. A nod to the waitress as I come in, that I'm headed outside to the bar and promptly waved on by.

Strolling on past the families that are gathered together and walking out to the outer deck outside past the signs that say DON"T FEED THE ALIGATORS!! Picking a spot, a cold beer you settle in to listen to the bands and watch the sunset over the bay.

There Teresa will greet you with a smile and a cold beer and stories of growing up on the bay. One particular evening the subject of change came up.

 I see people change every day, some wishing things would change and some changes happening to some that are lost with no direction.

What will I do now, is often said. Most of the time we're waiting on others to change thinking this will somehow make our life complete. Change will not come if we wait for some other person or some other time. We are the ones we've been waiting for. We are the change that we really need to focus on. You ever thought, what would happen if I change? Hmmm might make everything else change too.

Remember, if we don't change, we don't grow. If we don't grow, we aren't really living.

Put a smile on enjoy your day and weekend and if you really wanted to change it, well you would

Good Morning.

Meanwhile looking out at the sunrise from Pelican Cove down in Key Largo one time, watching the sail boat makers push the new sail boats into the water for their maiden voyages.

Each sailboat has a promise of smiles from its crew and new silk sails of bright colors. Each sailboat has its own unique character, feel and smoothness as it goes off in search of the breeze on Mother Ocean.

As they sit there, gentle rocking back and forth waiting, all the chrome shinning in the morning light I'm reminded of how sailboats and promises, people and dreams are all one in the same.

We all, like the sailboats start out with great promise, life is just a breeze along the way storms come and go but we sail on. Life will bring you to deep dark waters, self-pity; hatred and anger will drown you in the water of emotions but with acceptance, forgiveness, and love you can rise up to surface.

With focus, determination, and endurance you can sail back to the shore where the new triumphed and undefeated "you" is waiting to greet you.

Life is a breeze as long as you decide to sail, that's all nothing more Have a great day.

Good Morning.

Meanwhile, as traveler over the years you learn certain things about the road and why it calls you. I remember my dad talking about the people and places he had seen before he finally hung up his traveling shoes, only to live out the rest of his life telling traveling stories, there we're always stories. The road does keep you moving on and slowly disappears in your mirrors.

One should always move in a forward direction, don't get caught up in what you've left behind don't waste your time on those who had their chances and blew it. Stop focusing on what you don't want to happen. Focus on what you do want to happen. Positive thinking is at the forefront of every great success story. If you awake every morning with the thought that something wonderful will happen in your life today, and you pay close attention, you'll often find that you're right.

Remember, No matter how bad or good you have it, wake up each day thankful for your life. Someone somewhere else is desperately fighting for theirs. Instead of thinking about what you're missing, try thinking about what you do have that everyone else is missing out on

Have an awesome day.

Good Morning.

Meanwhile, down on Marco Island originally named San Marco Island by Spanish explorers, Marco Island is the largest barrier island within Southwest Florida's Ten Thousand Islands area extending southerly to Cape Sable. When Spanish explorers came to the island in the mid-1500s, they gave the island the name "La Isla de San Marco" after gospel writer St. Mark

There you'll find the sugar white sands of Tigertail Beach, Florida. I stumbled across the lure and magic of the islands purely by accident a few years ago and fell in love with the lagoon that naturally separates itself from Mother Ocean.

On the eastside is Tigertail Beach Café, a popular Marco Island restaurant for locals and tourists alike overlooking the beautiful lagoon of Tigertail Beach Park.

There one morning the subject of changes and life's surprises came up.

It's funny how all the planning in the world can't stop the clock on the wall, tick, tick, tick… One has to be careful to not to plan yourself out of today, meaning that the reason you planned a year ago was to live today. Life has a way of testing a person's will, either by having nothing happen at all or by having everything happen at once, so you have to be ready.

Life is strange; you never know who is going to come in and out of your life, what experiences will come in and out of your life, and just when you think you have it all figured out life comes at you and takes you by surprise. You never know what's in store for you the next day. However that's also the fun part change is good. Change keeps your mind on your life and not the tick, tick, tick.

 Summer is around the corner, may the summer wind chimes bring you much joy, just remember to enjoy every minute of it, laugh, spend time with those who matter the most and always leave the door open for new friends and people who are meant to be there and not part of your plan.

 Have an awesome day.

Thank you Summer for all those summer days.

Good Morning

 Meanwhile, If you ever head north up the eastern coast through Virginia making your way along the coastline on the Currituck Banks Peninsula at the northern end of the Outer Banks, without knowing it there is the sleepy community of Sandbridge, Virginia Beach, Virginia. Sandbridge is known for its somewhat remote location and receives a smaller volume of visitors than the main Virginia Beach resort strip located a few miles to its north.

There you'll find Katie's Coffee shop next to the 3rd St. pier. Katie grew up in San Francisco and was married most of her life. She always had a dream of having a coffee shop by the beach. When her husband passed away a few years ago she sold everything got in her husband's favorite car a 1970 Chevelle 454 SS convertible, strawberry red and "bad ass" as she describes it . She put the top down and drove across the country to the east coast and once she saw the ocean she said this is home.

The coffee shop is full of charm of course like Katie with an apartment upstairs overlooking the beach. She spends her days working in her garden and laughing with her new friends, some say she should run for Mayor, hmmm maybe she says.

She reminds me of how people need to stop thinking they're not ready to live, move on or go for a new opportunity.

Nobody ever feels 100% ready when an opportunity arises. Because most great opportunities in life force us to grow beyond our comfort zones, which means we won't feel totally comfortable at first.

However growing and changing is part of the movie we're all in, so we have to embrace these little changes. Don't worry about what others are doing better than you.

Concentrate on beating your own records every day. Success is a battle between YOU and YOURSELF only that's all

Have a great day and check out an old song by Oasis called "Don't look back in Anger"

Good Morning.

If you travel down Galt Ocean Dr. down in Fort Lauderdale, FL on the Atlantic coast about 20 miles north of Miami you begin to feel the history of the area if you venture off the touristy Ocean Blvd. There you'll find Ocean Manor Tiki Bar, where Janice who oversees the goings and comings of the best Tiki bar on the beach is and one who loves the history of Fort Lauderdale.

I remember writing the story of William Cooley on a napkin one afternoon as the sun was going down sipping on a cold Land shark beer. The story went this way.

The Fort Lauderdale area was known as the "New River Settlement" before the 20th century. In the 1830s there were about 70 settlers living along the New River, she says. William Cooley, the local Justice of the Peace, was a farmer and wrecker, who traded with the Seminole Indians. One day as fate would have it in 1836, while Cooley was leading an attempt to salvage a wrecked ship, a band of Seminoles attacked his farm, killing his wife and children, and the children's tutor. The other farms in the settlement were not attacked, but all the residents in the area abandoned the settlement, fleeing first to the Cape Florida Lighthouse on Key Biscayne, and then to Key West.

The first United States stockade named Fort Lauderdale was built in 1838 and subsequently was a site of fighting during the Second Seminole War.

The fort was abandoned in 1842, after the end of the war, and the area remained virtually unpopulated until the 1890s.

I love these stories of the past and how people made it through these situations. One can only imagine how places like Fort Lauderdale and other beaches where in the past with small towns and no cars, trains or traffic, just beaches and Mother Ocean constantly changing the coastline.

One of the things I say often is for everything you win you always loose something, figuring out if what you're winning is worth what your loosing is the key to long term happiness. I stop striving a long time ago for perfection, and have long ago forgiven myself for the mistakes I've made. For me knowing who I am, the friends and family that matter the most and living for today is the tradeoff for what I may have lost forever looking for perfection.

Whatever you do live in the moment, love like there's no tomorrow and always take time for strangers and friends alike along the way.

Have an awesome day and remember the reason one door closes and one opens is life's way of pushing you through to where you're supposed to be, the trick is to be willing to go through the door

Have a great day.

Good Morning.

Meanwhile, back to the island of sailboats where the makers, handcrafters and artist work their craft, shaping and molding the wood building the magic for a smooth ride the craft is always the same. No doubt there will be trouble waters and storms she will have to sail in but she sails on in search of the breeze and the magic of Mother Ocean and the sunny days, mornings and sunsets her bright colors will shine in.

If you worry about the storms one may never see the sunsets.

Remember throughout time in the confrontation between the stream and the rock, the stream always wins; not through strength, but through persistence.

Perseverance is the key. Isn't it funny how day by day nothing changes, but when you look back everything is different?" I stop waiting on ships to come in long ago I've found its better If your ship doesn't come in to swim out to meet it

Have an awesome day.

Good Morning.

 The waters, inlets and coves surrounding Florida's coasts have been the refuge of infamous pirates for centuries. From pillaging Spanish galleons carrying gold to Civil War blockade runners disrupting supply lines, the pirates of Florida were once feared and respected. Navigating tempestuous waters from Fort Myers down to Sanibel and Captiva Islands, south to Naples and east to the coveted Keys, these pirates and privateers embodied freedom and adventure. They secured their places in history while fighting the likes of presidents, armadas and international powers.

Did you know they were woman pirates? It's true. Mary Read was an English pirate. She and Anne Bonny are two of the most famed female pirates of all time; they are the only two women known to have been convicted of piracy during the early 18th century, at the height of the Golden Age of Piracy.

 Read's ship was taken by pirates, who forced her to join them. She took the King's pardon and took a commission to privateer, until that ended with her joining the crew in mutiny. In 1720 she joined pirate John "Calico Jack" Rackham and his companion, the female pirate Anne Bonny.

Rackham and his crew were arrested and brought to trial in what is now known as Spanish Town, Jamaica, where they were sentenced to hang for acts of piracy, as were Read and Bonny. However, the women escaped the noose when they revealed they were both "quick with child" (known as "Pleading the belly"), so they received a temporary stay of execution, she later died in prison but no record of any baby was ever noted.

Makes me think of why you should never give up EVER! Fear is a habit; so is self-pity, defeat, anxiety, despair, hopelessness and resignation.

You can eliminate all of these negative habits with two simple resolves: I can!! And I will!!"

Remember at the end of the day you really wanted to change it, well you would

Have a great day.

Good Morning.

Meanwhile down in Southwest Florida which extends from Anna Maria Island on the south side of Tampa Bay down to Marco Island in the southern end of the state. Where the northern stretch of the west coast of Florida is protected by barrier islands and it is on those islands or keys that you will find the beaches and most of the beach bars. Although this is a long stretch of coastline, bars are far and few between.

There you'll find Lido Key Tiki Bar which is a classic Florida beach bar formerly known as Azure Tides. It is Sarasota's only beachfront Tiki bar. The Tiki Bar sits right on the beach there is a fire pit on the beach for winter sunsets and gatherings and time to relax.

In the morning time if you go past the pier where the fisherman are gathering in search of the catch of the day and adventures for those who dare to go, you can sit in the blue chair and absorb the day

Watching the sunrises slowly turning the light to brightness and a sharp crisp in the air as the sounds of the beach begin to take over and the day begins.

Janice works the chalk board and its creativeness of different colors for her daily drink specials, out on the ocean the boats are off on their adventures as the beach comer helicopter flies overhead pulling the latest tourist banner.

There the subject of uncertainty came up.

Once again the changes of your life are like the calendar's page being turned, as if a way to keep up with how far you've came and how far you have to go. These changes are like dominos, once one falls they all fall. This can be sparked by a new relationship, one ending, a new job or change of residence.

One day you look up and everything has changed.

Sometimes worrying about tomorrow so much will cause you to miss the happiness today may bring. With that said one must stop running from your problems and accept the changes face them head on. No, it won't be easy.

There is no person in the world capable of flawlessly handling every punch thrown at them. We aren't supposed to be able to instantly solve problems. That's not how we're made. In fact, we're made to get upset, sad, hurt, stumble and fall. Because that's the whole purpose of living to face problems, learn, adapt, and solve them over the course of time. This is what ultimately molds us into the person we become.

Have an awesome day and remember you only have one today.

Good Morning.

Meanwhile, there are many places in the Deep South where beauty and charm meet, where history is rich and the people make the place and pull you into their culture.

Some take you to another place and time and the history will overwhelm you and capture your heart about the stories of those who walked the rock streets, covered bridges and fought the battles almost like threads woven into an old blanket your grandmother once made for you, even now if you cover up with it you're right back there.

 Just the mention of the name of some places can pull you into them and touch your soul Savanah, New Orleans, Charleston; they all are as they sound.

Traveling down highway 17 half-way between Myrtle Beach and Charleston South Carolina, is a beautiful old charm waterfront community easily accessible by land or sea. There you'll find Georgetown, South Carolina and is the third oldest city in the U.S.

Georgetown occupies a unique place in American history. Some historians claim that American history began here in 1526 with the earliest settlement in North America by Europeans. The stories are not always good as most cities dating that far back are victims of themselves with greed and a never-ending desire for power, still, the beauty is there as if God stopped one day and painted a portrait to last forever.

One particular morning making my way down Front Street in an area also known as "Little Charleston" where the second largest seaport along the coast can be found. The morning sunshine was lightning up the tables and umbrellas outside The Dogwood Café as the curtains wave back and forth from the ocean breeze.

Contessa is in one of the many rooms of tall ceilings that appear to be a dining room once upon a time as the house itself dates back to the 18th century. She's wearing a long white dress and has long black hair that is curly and pulled back and she is grating cheeses for the lunch specials.

There is a tall hour glass turned upside down she uses as a clock for a two hour time, the sand creating a pyramid of time.

There the subject of want to do's vs have to do's came up.

It's funny how one reaches decisions by simply stopping to take a snap shot of where you are, where you want to go and a sudden importance put on by the awareness of just how much time has passed.

If you reach the point to where you do things because you want to and not because you have to, it does put a whole new light on things.

Decisions about relationship's, careers can bring you a sense of change is needed, yes a change is needed.

As the sand continues to pile up in the hour glass the thought of desire and what one brings to the table comes to mind.

Remember, desire is the one element you must always bring to the table, if you don't have it, no one can give it to you. Beware of the road blocks and ask yourself, "Is this a good fit for me?" "Will this bring me the passion I need?" and it's ok to think about yourself for a change?

All the sand has gone now and the cheeses have all been granted, it's time to move on now

Have a great day.

Good Morning.

Meanwhile, earlier in the year I took off for a week for a much needed time away like a verse out of Jimmy Buffett's changes in latitudes, changes in attitudes song the intent was to get away and reflect on the last 5 years. The water was warm but not summer ready yet as it splashed and crawled its way to the sand, the new season of summer and promise was poised to begin I thought about this chapter of my life.

If you've followed my writings before then you know that a chapter in your life is 5 years and what a difference 5 years can make if you stop to reflect on it.

Sitting and watching one day the sun rise across the ocean like a new chapter beginning I thought of the people around me and how much they've changed, the people that have come and gone and the places from which I've traveled.

The most important thing is to focus on how much you've changed, is it for the better? Are you moving forward? Never underestimate the power of asking yourself these two important questions.

 Like a sailboat on the ocean all the parts working together to move you forward, we are our own sails. In Chattanooga they've erected a wall called "Before I die" a movement across the country with lines on it of things to accomplish, a bucket list if you will.

I thought about how we really don't need a movement to make these list and how simple some of these really are and one should always have that list in mind at all times.

Like the waves that day on the beach or the sailboat sailing each choice we make causes a ripple effect in our lives. When things happen to us, it is the reaction we choose that can create the difference between the sorrow of our past and the joy in our future.

I choose to be happy and sail on in search of the breeze. Now turn the page a new chapter has begun

Have an awesome day.

Good Morning.

Meanwhile, the summer of 1622 in Panama City was a busy time for the ship. Most of her precious cargo arrived by mule and took 2 months to record and load. After she left Panama City bound for Havana the now famous pride of Spain sailed to meet her convoy that was to depart for Spain on September 4th 1622, six weeks behind schedule. At this very moment the perfect storm was moving its way across the ocean at high speed just a short 200 miles away,

Like a hurricane of events leading to a deadly and disastrous ending effecting many lives and Spain forever, the mother ship Atocha sailed into history unaware of her fate.

Two days later on the 6th of September the Atocha was driven by a severe hurricane onto the coral reefs about 35 miles west of Key West. With her hull badly damaged, she quickly sank, drowning everyone on board except for three sailors and two slaves. A second hurricane in October of that year made attempts at salvage even more difficult by scattering the wreckage of the ship still further as Mother Ocean had claimed her for her own determined to keep her.

The discovery of the Ghost Ship as described by those who discouraged the finding of The Atocha is as fascinating as the story of the ship herself.

Most people would never know the story of the famed ship if not for an American treasure hunter named Mel Fisher who after 16 ½ years finally discovered The Atocha on July 20th 1985.

The discovery of the lost ship came at a price for Mel along the way many times over including the loss of his son and his wife who died in one of the capsized salvage ships shortly after finding pieces of the ship in 1975. Still Mel sailed on and believed in his dream as if it was destiny that brought the ship and Mel to find each other.

Shortly after the discovery the state of Florida tried to claim it for its own which eventually led to the Supreme Court ruling in Mel's favor after eight years of litigation. Once again Mel stayed the course.

The more you read of these events and the story of Mel's life the more you realize what true determination really is and why the importance of following your dreams is so important. Doing something and getting it wrong is at least ten times more productive than doing nothing. Remember, every success has a trail of failures behind it, and every failure is leading towards success.

You end up regretting the things you did NOT do far more than the things you did.

Mel Fisher started each day with the promise of

"*Today is the day*" that the treasure would be found and so it was found.

You're treasure is waiting for you and today is the day to begin. Don't allow your dreams to slip away another day.

Today is the day!

Have an awesome adventure in search of your life and your dreams.

Danny Lynn

The Tiki Man.

Notes

Notes

Notes